Toxic Grief of Helen Samson

By Connie Smith

First Edition

By Connie Smith

©2009, 2015 by Connie Smith

Edited by Carlie Mae and Lilly Sherman

ISBN: 978-1-329-71863-0

Table of Contents

Disclaimer

The following story is based on facts, but the names of persons, businesses, and communities (along with their locations) were changed to protect their identities. Therefore, any likeness of any of the names in this book to any known individuals, businesses, or communities is purely coincidental.

Connie Smith

Definition

Toxic -- The word "toxic" means that something is destructive or harmful in such a way that the toxic substance inhibits the normal activity, course of reaction, or process of another substance. Through its chemical action, a toxic substance can kill, injure, or impair a vulnerable organism.

Chapter 1: Helen Samson

This is a story about a special friend named Helen Samson, who came into my life almost 8 years ago. She was being poisoned by her grief of 33 years over the death of her husband DeWayne. She was so poisoned by her grief that it had impaired her mind and body to the point where she had no vision for life, and she was simply waiting to die.

First, let me tell you who Helen Samson is. She is now 70 years old. She is a highly intelligent woman who has a

Bachelor's Degree in Nursing and a Master's Degree in Counseling. She is of medium height and slightly overweight with dark hair that is showing some gray. She is very good-looking, and she has a wonderful sense of humor, which began to show up soon after the beginning of the healing process.

Moreover, Helen has a beautiful spirit: She is very open-minded, and she loves the Lord with all her heart. She is a very loving being, full of light; and I am so glad that God brought her across my path.

Helen retired from her job as a Registered Nurse on November 30, 2007, and she, then, became almost a recluse in her home. She rarely socialized, and she

2

visited mostly with her mother, who *likewise* was grieving somewhat over the death of her *own* husband. Hence, at the time, Helen and her mother had a lot in common: their *grief*.

Chapter 2: Tools for Healing

Prior to our first meeting, Helen had read an article in a magazine about Vibrational Sound Therapy. At the time, she was going to ***"Massage and Therapy by Design,"*** which is owned by a woman named Lydia Stobel. She asked Lydia if she (Lydia) had heard anything about Vibrational Sound Therapy, whereupon Lydia referred her to me.

Vibrational Sound Therapy is a tool for healing that is completely natural. It is very useful in clearing emotional blockages. These blockages are made up of emotional thought-patterns and old-belief structures. They cause *tension* in the *mind* similar to a cold draft or an injury can cause muscular tension in the *body*. These emotional blockages resist consciousness and require higher vibration to break this vicious cycle. (Sound Healing with the Five Elements, by Daniel Perret.)

Since sound is non-physical, we need to understand that the body can be restored to balance through non-physical means. Vibrational Sound Healing works with the energy fields of the body. Energy fields exist around everything in the world, including *humans*, and vibrations from certain harps can penetrate these energy fields. Therefore, such vibrations can be used to neutralize energy disturbances that are caused by emotional blockages.

Music affects people in different ways: It can elevate the spirit; it can be depressing; it can be inspirational. The use of sound for healing purposes is a re-emerging technique-and-science that is based on Sympathetic Vibratory Physics. The science of sound healing existed in the past, as ancients used such tools as Tibetan singing-bowls, drums, and didgeridoos (Australian Aborigine musical instrument made from a long wooden tube that produces a low drone sound.) Once lost to us, this technology is now resurging.

In any event, in April of 2008, Helen called me and made an appointment for Vibrational Sound Healing, which is a work that God gave me to do as well as gifting me the tools to do it. Most of all, *God* is the real Gift, and it is *He* who directs every session: I am only His *Worker*.

God placed in my life two very special instruments: I have two precious harps that are about the size of *auto harps*, and they were anointed by God. Whenever someone comes for help, I pray and ask God for direction, and He answers me.

The harps were developed through a revelation that was given to a woman named Rev. Barbie Edwards in Colorado.

They were prayed over before they were sold, and a Spirit Guide was sent with each harp.

One is the *Indian Harp* (Native American Harp), which is made of Redwood. It is very beautiful, and it plays in a *minor* key. The other is the *Angel Harp*. It is white; it is decorated with figures of angels; and it plays beautifully in a *major* key.

God sends me *help* whenever I play the harps. With the *Indian Harp*, an attractive Indian *warrior* appears as a guide when I play it. With the *Angel Harp*, a beautiful *angel* ministers to the client as I play it.

Led by God's Spirit, I play the harp with my eyes closed. With each person, the music comes out *differently*, as each person is so unique.

These harps are harmonized to touch every energy level of the body and energize each Chakra. According to believers, there are seven main Chakras, which are openings (or "energy centers") in the human body.

Dr. Valerie Hunt, who has researched the healing aspects of Sound Therapy, believes that the tunings of the harps raise the coherency in the energy fields of the body, which helps us to heal. Every note of these instruments vibrates at a specific frequency, and the different frequencies affect the different layers of energy fields in a person's body.

The process in music and sound therapy activates the subconscious of the client and allows that client to bring the subconscious into the open so that healing can occur.

According to the inventor of the harps (Rev. Barbie Edwards), many receive advanced states of meditation and deep relaxation with the angelic tuning of the harp. The Indian harp is used during the first portion of the treatment to align the lower three Chakras of the body, which is based on earth-energy/Native American.

A growing number of scientific publications document how music may be helpful in:

1. Lowering the blood pressure

2. Enhancing the immune system

3. Raising the blood oxygen level

4. Lowering the heart rate

5. Improving the circulation

6. Reducing tension in muscles

7. Lowering fear levels

8. Decreasing sleeping difficulties

9. Lowering physical pain levels

10. Cleansing the energy centers and the auras

In addition to the harps, I have a number of "Young Essential Oils." God tells me which oils to use and where to apply them on the body. These oils are for emotions: They shift the client's vibration and help him (or her) to open up so that he (or she) can receive the healing from God.

These are the tools that I used with Helen Samson.

Chapter 3: The Therapy

When Helen walked through my
doorway on April 21, 2008, she
resembled a walking *dead* person: She
had no light in her eyes, no spring in her
steps, and no reason to live. Furthermore,
she was taking the anti-depressants Zoloft
and Wellbutrin just to keep going. The
medication was helping her, but she was
living her life in a fog.

As with any new client, I instructed
Helen to fill out a form for basic
information, and I had her sign a release

at the bottom of the page. On the form, I asked several questions, and one of them was, "What problems do you hope to correct through the therapy?"

Helen answered, "To lift depression and enjoy life more."

Helen would certainly get her wishes. On the first day, I said many things to Helen that frightened her, and even though she had much fear, she was desperate enough to continue the healing process. Helen also felt that God had *led* her to me, which gave her *further* encouragement.

Incidentally, to some extent, *most* of us are afraid of concepts that are new or unfamiliar to us. Only the extremely confident or the foolhardy experience no fear.

Anyway, Helen remained faithful to come for her monthly sessions. As mentioned above, Helen's desire for getting well was greater than her fears, and therefore she bravely continued with the sessions.

We worked together faithfully at least once a month, and little by little, with each session, God revealed important things to us. He directed every session, and with each step and with each revelation, Helen slowly showed signs of healing.

Many past lives came forth as Helen's healing connected to the root of her mourning, which her spirit had clung to since the year 1750. Yes, we *all* have lived before, and that was a hard point for Helen, because she had lived in a very traditional Church setting where such things are not taught. However, thank God for Helen's open-mindedness, for if she had not been willing to receive such information, she would not be healed today.

In any case, every month, I was greatly encouraged by Helen's progress, and I learned so much from what God revealed during each session. Sometimes we laughed, and sometimes we cried; but by the end of the session, we always rejoiced at the progress that Helen was making.

Twice, I felt led to do "Past-Life Regression" with Helen, and with each Regression period, Helen realized a great deal of healing. Hence, Past-Life Regression proved to be an effective tool in bringing Helen out of the past and into the present.

In July of 2008, Helen informed me that she had forgotten to take the medication Wellbutrin, and she felt so much *better*. Therefore, she felt that she no longer *needed* that particular medication, and she stopped taking it.

Then, when Helen came for her *August* session, she told me that she herself had lowered her Zoloft from 200mg to 50mg, and she was doing just fine. She explained that, as she was trying to take her pills one evening, the *Zoloft* tablet seemed to jump right out of her mouth, and so she decided to *lower* the dosage of that particular medication.

Incidentally, I *never* advise anyone to discontinue his (or her) medication: Helen discontinued the medication on her *own*!

Anyway, a lot of material was revealed during this particular session. We were shown that, when we continue to grieve and mourn a person's death, we hold his (or her) spirit in this lower plane (i.e., in a third dimension). The spirit cannot leave for a higher plane if we continue to hold onto things that the deceased once had possessed (especially if the item has the deceased's *blood* on it, for the blood is the *life force* of the body). Furthermore, the spirits of the deceased have *tasks* to do on the other side, and they cannot go and perform the tasks until we *release* them.

The Holy Spirit instructed Helen and me to do a "Clean Sweep" in Helen's home. Helen had accumulated many things, and she was holding onto many things that were connected to her husband DeWayne. Helen's heart was telling her that, in her Toxic Grief, she somehow was holding onto her husband *DeWayne* by holding onto his *things.*

DeWayne's spirit (in human form) would come through in each session, and he would beg Helen to let him go: She was holding him in a third dimension by holding onto the items in her home, in her heart, and in her mind.

Whenever the spirit appeared to me, he wore the same clothing in which he was killed: He was a motorcycle racer, and he was killed during a race. Helen had held onto his helmet, bag, shirts, wedding paraphernalia, his ashes in the cremation box, his yearly calendar, the memorial book from his funeral service, etc.

On the helmet, there was *blood* from DeWayne's death, and when that fact was revealed to me, I immediately knew that Helen could not just throw the helmet into the trash: The blood would have to be *burned*, because there was a strong connection between DeWayne's spirit (still present in the physical world) and the dried blood. Helen and I did not understand such knowledge at the time, but we would understand it later.

In any event, Helen worked diligently through the next 3 months doing the Clean Sweep, and she completely cleaned, organized, gave away, and discarded many things except *DeWayne's* items.

Meanwhile, in September, when Helen arrived for her regular session, she had been off the Zoloft for 3 weeks, and she was doing *wonderfully*. She was waking up and coming alive again, and it was so *marvelous* to see the improvement.

God is always so *wonderful* to all of us, and He knows how to lead us in the right steps if we only would *listen*. In the case of Helen Samson, for example, she *listened*, and she had good results. Not everyone can succeed, but in *Helen's* case, God was leading her, and she understood and responded appropriately.

Then, in November, there was a huge breakthrough. DeWayne's spirit appeared with his *mother's* spirit. (She had died the year before.) Because *DeWayne's* spirit was confined to the third dimension, his *mother's* spirit was confined to the third dimension as well, for she was concerned over her son, and she felt that she could not leave without him. Obviously, Helen's grieving was not only holding back *DeWayne's* spirit, but it was also holding back DeWayne's *mother's* spirit. Hence, Helen and I could see very clearly that DeWayne's items were preventing *two* spirits from ascending to the higher plane.

On this particular day, we knew that we were getting down to the "nitty-gritty" so to speak. It was emotionally an extremely painful session for Helen, and I had to counsel her very carefully as to what the next step would be.

God revealed that Helen could simply give away or discard all the items except the *helmet*, which would have to be *burned*: The burning would *release* the deceased's spirit so that it, at last, could ascend. In essence, by burning the helmet, Helen would be completely changing the composition of the helmet so that the deceased's spirit could be released completely.

In the past, Helen always had been a procrastinator, and she had great difficulty finishing anything that she started. However, with this healing process, she definitely wanted to finish it.

She did have a certain amount of fear about finishing the job: What would she do *afterward*? After all, she was *accustomed* to the mourning and the grieving; and even though they were *unhealthy* for her, they were *familiar* to her, which gave her a sense of *security* to a certain degree.

DeWayne's spirit expressed that Helen had *no idea* as to how much power the items had: They were powerful enough to prevent him from ascending, especially the helmet with his *blood* on it, and he begged Helen to let him go.

Therefore, to get rid of the items and allow the deceased's spirit to ascend, Helen did some weeping that day, and I reassured her that I would stand with her all the way. If she should need me, I would gladly go to her home and help her to gather the items and travel with her to anywhere that she would choose for the burning. Helen was greatly comforted by my offer.

I advised Helen not to get depressed when she went home. Instead, she should continue the Clean Sweep little by little until the job was completed.

Therefore, by the time she left for home, Helen had begun to accept the fact that she truly needed to complete the Clean Sweep and burn the helmet, and she felt that she knew where she could carry out the burning. She thought of a field that was located approximately 15 miles north of town, and she believed that the burning should take place in that particular field.

Then, before the next session, Helen learned some important things that were pertinent to the burning of the items. She learned that the field she needed was not available. Therefore, she and her mother took a ride and saw *another* field that appeared to be suitable for the burning. Next, as Helen and her mother were looking at the field, a man approached them and claimed that he knew the owner of the field. So, Helen politely asked the man if he thought it would be okay for her to burn some old mementos in the field, and the man replied, "Sure, that would be no problem." However, we would later learn that the man's friendly attitude was not reflecting the attitude of the field's *owner*.

Meanwhile, for several months prior to the burning of the items, Helen had been receiving a form of alternative medicine called "Reiki" from a woman named Monica Lang.

Reiki was developed in 1922 by a Japanese Buddhist named Mikao Usui. Its technique involves *palm healing* or

hands-on healing, and it is believed that
the therapist transfers "universal energy"
through his (or her) palms to the client,
which encourages healing.

In any case, the treatments had
helped Helen greatly, and she had become
close to Monica *personally*. Then, in
December, as Monica was administering
the Reiki treatment to Helen, she
(Monica) received a revelation that she
should go to the burning.

Originally, Helen and I thought that
I would be the only one to accompany
Helen to the burning. So apparently, God
must have brought all three of us together
to complete the burning of the items.
Each one of us would contribute a
necessary part of the process of burning

28

the items so that Helen could release DeWayne's spirit and allow him to ascend to a higher plane.

Before the burning, Helen came to me for her regular session on December 15, 2008. I applied the necessary oils to her body and placed the Indian Harp on her chest and abdomen.

Then, a few minutes later, a sudden *fear* came upon Helen. It was the fear of *change* or the fear of the *unknown*. The dimension in which Helen had lived was very low and depressing. Nevertheless, it was *familiar*, which meant that Helen knew what to expect every day. Now, however, everything was about to change, and Helen did not know how the change would affect her. Therefore, Helen, at first, feared and resisted the change and the unknown.

Helen voiced her fear, and we dealt with it and continued the session with great joy and peace. During the session, God instructed Helen to read the Bible and other positive books (that evening) to remain focused for the next day: The next day would be December 16, the day on which the burning of the items was scheduled to take place.

We made plans for Helen to pick up Monica and me at my house at 9:30 a.m., and we would travel together to the field with the supplies and the items.

Helen went home and had quite a night while preparing for the next day. She had wept very heavily when her husband DeWayne was killed in the motorcycle race, but she did not weep at all during the Memorial Service. So that night, she told God, "I want to feel the pain of the loss, really feel it, for I have been numb for so long."

God answered her prayer: She, later, told Monica and me that she had wept heavily most of the night, and it was deep, *deep* weeping.

As for me, at 3:00 a.m., I was awakened by DeWayne's spirit. He was extremely excited about the upcoming burning, for he knew that it would be his homecoming. He was so full of joy that he just could not contain himself, and he was literally *dancing* all around my house. He seemed to be so *thrilled* of being so close to getting out of this (third) dimension. After all, he had been earthbound for 33 years.

The spirit gave me instructions for the next day: Helen, Monica, and I must wear *pink*, which represents the "Heart Chakra." It is connected to the emotion of *Love*.

As mentioned earlier, the human body has seven main Chakras, which are openings (or "energy centers") for the "life energy" to flow into and out of our aura. Life energy affects physical, mental, and emotional health. Some believers and therapists (including the author) believe that the color "pink" represents the Heart Chakra, while others believe that the color "green" represents the Heart Chakra.

In any case, at the burning, we must face *eastward*, as that direction represents the within and the place of the dawning of a new day. Then, when the fire would touch the blood on the helmet, we would see DeWayne's spirit ascend: The spirit would ascend in the smoke just as *God* is represented in the smoke many times in the Scripture.

At this point, God intervened and explained that Helen *personally* must place the items on the fire. By doing so, she would burn away (some say "balance") approximately 500 years of karma. She would burn away many lifetimes of mourning and trauma.

Furthermore, the cells of Helen's body would change, because the karma is held in the cells of the body. Therefore, after the karma has been destroyed, Helen would experience a great shift in her body.

Anyway, DeWayne's spirit and I saw the spirit of DeWayne's father (who had passed away many years earlier) reaching down for the spirt of DeWayne's mother. The father's spirit was waiting on the other side for the *mother's* spirit; and the mother's spirit, in turn, was staying for their *son's* spirit. Meanwhile, the son's spirit was waiting for Helen to let him go. As a result, the *father's* spirit could not move on and evolve.

We, then, saw DeWayne's spirit and his *mother's* spirit; and behind them, there was a great crowd of spirits. They looked at us and asked, "When will it be *our* turn? Could you please *help* us?" The entire crowd of spirits was stranded in the third dimension because someone's *grieving* was keeping them earthbound.

I immediately thought of the Scripture in Hebrews 12:1 where it reads that we are encompassed about with this great cloud of witnesses. I truly believe that we saw the cloud of witnesses in that vision.

In any event, shortly after dawn, the sky was bright and clear. It was a cold day, something like 17 degrees, and we were all dressed in layers. However, the roads were clear and dry, and no snow was predicted.

Meanwhile, DeWayne's spirit had stayed with me since 3:00 a.m., because he knew that he should stay close to me so that Helen would go through with the burning.

Helen arrived at my house around 9:40 a.m., and as we had planned, we all wore "pink." The three of us (Helen, Monica, and I) rode in Helen's car to the field where we were to burn the items. We arrived at the field around 10:00 a.m., and we proceeded to unload the equipment and the items for the burning.

Incidentally, the *date* of the burning (12-16-08) contained significant numbers: The number "12" is the number of the redeemed; the number "16" is the number of love; and the number "8" is the number for a new beginning. (Number in Scripture, by E. W. Bullinger)

In any case, after we had carried all the things into the field, we noticed that there seemed to be *two* fields: One was near the road; the other one was in the back of the area. The field in the back was a beautiful circular setting among Birch trees, and it resembled a Native American camp. Therefore, we moved the things to the other field and readied everything for the burning. The setting was perfect: We could even *feel* the presence of Native American spirits as we began to prepare the fire.

We built the fire; we said a prayer; and we faced *eastward* as instructed. Next, I saturated some of the items with barbecue lighter fluid as Helen respectfully dropped them into the fire. There was a 5-10 miles-per-hour wind that morning, which naturally made the fire burn hotter and consume the items more quickly.

Then, as we were busily employed with our task, we happened to look up and noticed a truck that was pulling up at the edge of the field. A man got out and walked towards us with great determination. He approached us and asked, "What are you guys doing here?"

Helen replied, "I have permission to burn a few items here."

The man asked, "Who gave you the permission?"

Helen pointed toward a house across the field and replied, "A man that lives there."

The man said, "Well, he had no right to give you the permission, as it is not his property; it's *mine*."

The man, then, asked what we were burning, and Helen answered, "Just some mementos from my husband's death so that I can close out a chapter of my life."

Then, as soon as Helen had finished speaking, I intervened and explained that Helen was closing an *old* door and opening a *new* one, whereupon the man's aura and demeanor changed immediately.

He said, "All right. In that case, just clean things up when you're done."

I said, "Oh, thank you; God bless you."

The man, then, introduced himself as a builder in the area and shook our hands. We chatted with him for a few minutes and promised to clean things up before leaving.

He said, "Okay, ladies," and he wished Helen well and walked away.

After he left, we removed the helmet, the cremation box, and the memorial book from the bag. We burned the bag first. Then, Helen carefully placed the helmet into the fire.

When the fire touched the blood on the helmet, I immediately became aware of DeWayne's spirit ascending, just as God had promised. In addition, his *mother's* spirit became free to make her ascension, and we were aware of many angels all around us. We were also aware of many Native American spirits dancing around the fire. DeWayne's spirit ascended at 10:35 in the morning; he had his fatal accident almost 34 years earlier at 10:35 in the evening.

The burning was an amazing sight, for everything burned so *completely* that almost no ashes remained after the fire had burned out. We poured 5 bottles of water on the ashes to cool them so that we could put them in a bag. We, then, placed the bag of ashes in a box.

On the way home, we stopped at Helen's mother's house, for she was aware that we were burning the items, and she wanted to see us afterward.

We had a good visit. Helen's mother was so happy: Her daughter finally had gotten rid of the items that she had held onto for so long. We all had a cup of coffee and shared our love with her for a time before we left for home.

We were all deeply touched by the whole process of the burning, and we had learned lessons that only could be taught by God through His Spirit. What a mighty God we serve!

I believe that we all were aware of the presence of God during the burning process. I even shed *tears* during the process, and so did Monica. As for *Helen*, she already had wept deeply most of the night, and therefore she simply was ready to get it done.

It was a day that I will never forget. I never had done such a thing before during my entire time of ministry, which now spans 44 years. We never know what the Lord will ask of us to bring healing to someone else, so we must always be ready.

Helen is a different person today: She is alive; her eyes are full of light; her sense of humor is in full bloom; and she is full of joy.

When Helen came for her January session, everything that God had predicted was confirmed. In a vision, we saw all her former lives and all the spiritual beings that had come to each session. They were all dressed in white, and we understood what God had told us: The *karma* was gone because the *darkness* was gone.

We, then, saw Helen at a wedding, *her* wedding. All her attendants were angels dressed in white, and she was marrying "Fearless Witness."

Fearless Witness is neither a being nor a spirit: It is an *idea* that reflects Helen freeing herself from all her fears.

The marriage merged Helen and Fearless Witness into a single unit, and she became a powerful witness for God wherever she would go.

Helen was just *beginning* to live, and she now had a greater sense of knowing who she was and what she yet had to do.

Thank you, Father, for bringing Helen my way and using her life to teach me so many truths about the other side. She is a new sister in my life, and I love her very much.

Amen